Congressional
Research
Service

Controlling Air Emissions from Outer Continental Shelf Sources: A Comparison of Two Programs—EPA and DOI

Jonathan L. Ramseur
Specialist in Environmental Policy

November 26, 2012

Congressional Research Service

7-5700

www.crs.gov

R42123

Summary

Air emissions from outer continental shelf (OCS) operations are subject to different regulatory programs, depending on the location of the operation. The Department of the Interior (DOI) has jurisdiction over OCS sources in federal waters in the western Gulf of Mexico and most of the central Gulf. In addition, the Consolidated Appropriations Act, 2012 (P.L. 112-74), transferred air emission authority in the OCS off Alaska's north coast from the Environmental Protection Agency (EPA) to DOI. EPA has jurisdiction over sources in all other federal waters.

The primary difference between the EPA and DOI programs is rooted in the different statutory authorities: the 1990 Clean Air Act (CAA) and the 1978 Outer Continental Shelf Lands Act (OCSLA). The primary objectives of these statutes are different—air quality versus offshore energy development. The two regulatory programs reflect these underlying differences. For much of the past 30 years, these differences received little attention, primarily because most of the federal oil and gas resources in EPA's jurisdiction have been subject to moratoria. In 2008, moratoria provisions expired, potentially opening many of the areas in EPA's jurisdiction to oil and gas leasing activity. If more OCS areas in EPA's jurisdiction are open for oil and gas leasing, policymakers interest in these differences will likely increase.

For OCS sources in EPA's jurisdiction, requirements depend on whether the source is located within 25 miles of a state's seaward boundary ("inner OCS sources") or beyond ("outer OCS sources"). Inner OCS sources are subject to the same requirements as comparable onshore emission sources, which vary by state and depend on the area's air quality status; outer sources are subject to various CAA provisions, including the Prevention of Significant Deterioration (PSD) program. In contrast, OCS sources in DOI's jurisdiction are subject to air emission requirements only if emissions would "significantly affect" *onshore* air quality.

A key difference between the EPA and DOI programs is the federal emission threshold that would subject a source to substantive requirements. For sources in EPA's jurisdiction, this is the PSD threshold of 250 tons per year (tpy) of regulated emissions. Sources that exceed this level would likely be subject to Best Achievable Control Technology (BACT) and other provisions. States' analogous thresholds that apply to inner OCS sources may be more stringent. By comparison, a DOI OCS source applies an exemption formula, based on distance from shore (e.g., a source 30 miles from shore would have an emission threshold of 990 tpy). If a source remains subject after this step, it must conduct air modeling to assess whether its emissions would have a significant effect on onshore air quality. In effect, this two-step process constitutes a much less stringent threshold than EPA's 250 tpy threshold.

Another substantial difference is the time frame allotted to the agencies for reviewing a potential source's permit (EPA) or activity-specific plan (DOI). In addition, the EPA permit process allows greater opportunity for input from the public. In particular, EPA's Environmental Appeals Board offers parties a powerful tool to compel agency review.

Therefore, two identical operations, located in separate jurisdictions, could face considerably different requirements and procedural time frames. Some stakeholders would likely argue that the additional opportunities for public involvement in EPA's permit process help create a balance between resource development and environmental concerns. Others would likely contend these steps present unnecessary burdens and timing uncertainty in the process.

Contents

Figures

Tables

Contacts

Introduction

The same group of air pollutant emissions from outer continental shelf (OCS) operations are subject to different regulatory programs, depending on the location of the operation. The Department of the Interior (DOI) has jurisdiction over OCS sources in federal waters in the western Gulf of Mexico and most of the central Gulf. The Consolidated Appropriations Act, 2012 (P.L. 112-74), transferred air emission authority in the OCS off Alaska's north coast from the Environmental Protection Agency (EPA) to DOI. EPA has jurisdiction over sources in all other federal waters.

Reader's Note: DOI Delegation

DOI created the Minerals Management Service (MMS) in 1982.[1] On May 19, 2010, during the Deepwater Horizon oil spill response, the Secretary of DOI replaced MMS with the Bureau of Ocean Energy Management, Regulation and Enforcement (BOEMRE). On October 1, 2011, DOI divided BOEMRE into three separate entities: the Bureau of Ocean Energy Management (BOEM), the Bureau of Safety and Environmental Enforcement (BSEE), and Office of Natural Resources Revenue (ONRR). Both BOEM and BSEE have responsibilities that related to air emissions from OCS sources. A DOI October 2011 direct final rule explains how existing OCS regulations are now divided (or shared in some cases) between the two new agencies.[2]

Although MMS and BOEMRE no longer exist, this report refers to activities performed by these agencies during their existence. In addition, this report cites documents and websites that carry their names and are still valid.

Congress established the programs through different statutes, and the two agencies implement the programs through separate regulations. Pursuant to the underlying statutes, the regulations have different scopes, emission thresholds for eligibility, and compliance obligations.

Therefore, two identical operations, located in separate jurisdictions, could face considerably different requirements and procedural time frames. Some may criticize this arrangement for its inconsistent treatment of air emissions. Others may point out that the differences create inconsistent opportunities for oil and gas development.

For much of the past 30 years, these differences received little attention, primarily because most of the federal oil and gas resources in EPA's jurisdiction have been subject to moratoria. Moreover, the level of activities in the regions open to development has varied dramatically. According to DOI data from 2010, there were 3,409 *production* wells in the Gulf of Mexico and 23 in the Pacific.[3]

Figure 1 illustrates the divided jurisdiction in the Gulf of Mexico. Although active leases are located in EPA's jurisdiction, none of the Gulf of Mexico platforms are in EPA's jurisdiction.

---

[1] CRS Report R41485, *Reorganization of the Minerals Management Service in the Aftermath of the Deepwater Horizon Oil Spill*, by Henry B. Hogue.

[2] See 76 *Federal Register* 64432 (October 18, 2011).

[3] Bureau of Ocean Energy Management, "Installations and Removals - Offshore Production Facilities in Federal Waters Offshore Production Facilities in Federal Waters," at http://www.boem.gov/BOEM-Newsroom/Offshore-Stats-and-Facts/Offshore-Stats-and-Facts.aspx.

Figure 1. EPA and DOI OCS Air Emission Jurisdictions in the Gulf of Mexico

(red markers = active leases; green markers = platforms)

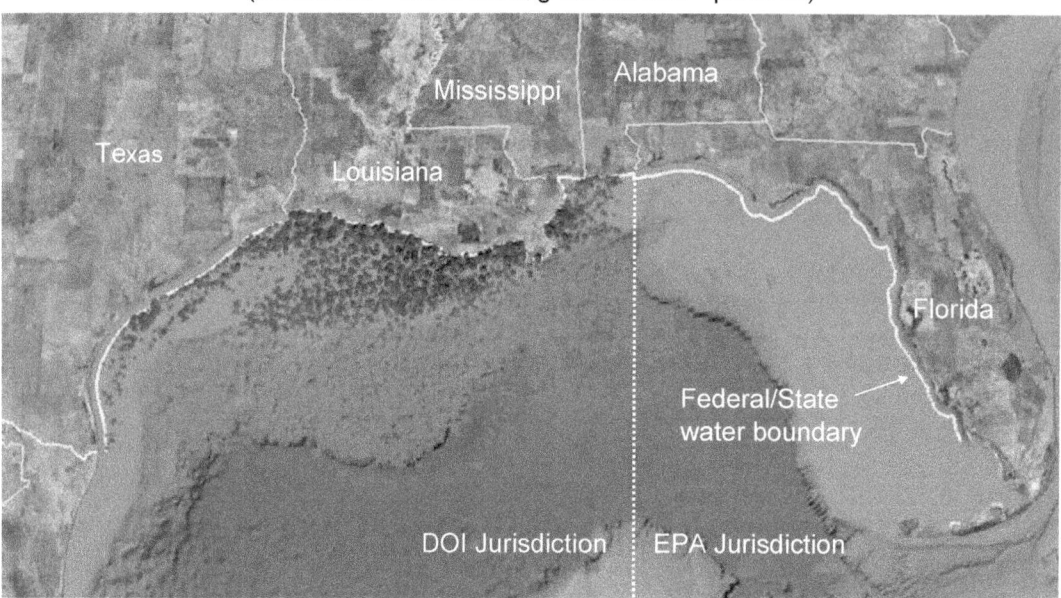

Source: Prepared by CRS; Active lease, platforms, and federal/state water boundary created Google Earth, using BOEMRE GIS files, at http://www.gomr.boemre.gov/homepg/data_center/geographic_mapping.html. Accessed data on October 3, 2011.

Notes: DOI has jurisdiction of OCS sources west of 87.5° longitude; EPA has jurisdiction east of this line. CRS inserted this line manually (in PowerPoint), so its position may not be precise.

In 2008, moratoria provisions expired, allowing many of the areas in EPA's jurisdiction to potentially open for oil and gas leasing activity. In addition, estimates of oil and gas resources have spurred interest in areas other than the Gulf (**Table 1**). For example, OCS areas off the Atlantic coast have also received attention in recent years. In 2007, the Minerals Management Service (MMS) proposed a lease sale in an area offshore of Virginia.[4] The lease sale was set to take place in 2011.[5] In the aftermath of the 2010 *Deepwater Horizon* oil spill, the Obama Administration canceled the sale (May 27, 2010).[6] In addition, in DOI's most recent five-year plan for OCS leasing, DOI decided not to include the Mid- and South Atlantic planning areas.[7]

Many Members of the 112th Congress have sought to expand OCS oil and gas development. The House has passed several bills[8] that would direct DOI to hold lease sales in particular areas, including the formerly proposed Virginia lease sale and areas of Southern California.

---

[4] After the 2010 Deepwater Horizon incident the MMS was replaced by the Bureau of Ocean Energy Management, Regulation and Enforcement (BOEMRE), which was subsequently divided into three separate entities: the Bureau of Ocean Energy Management (BOEM) and the Bureau of Safety and Environmental Enforcement (BSEE), and Office of Natural Resources Revenue (ONRR).

[5] See CRS Report R41132, *Outer Continental Shelf Moratoria on Oil and Gas Development*, by Curry L. Hagerty.

[6] For more information, see http://www.gomr.boemre.gov/homepg/lsesale/220/matl220.html.

[7] DOI, Bureau of Ocean Energy Management, Proposed Final Outer Continental Shelf Oil & Gas Leasing Program 2012-2017, June 2012, at http://www.boem.gov.

[8] For example, H.R. 1229, H.R. 1230, and H.R. 1231.

In addition, areas of the U.S. Arctic region, which were not subject to the moratoria, have generated recent congressional interest as industry has sought to establish a greater presence in the area.[9] A primary driver for the activity in this region is the shrinking Arctic ice cap, or conversely, the growing amount of ice-free ocean in the summertime.[10]

Table 1. Estimates of Oil and Gas Resources in U.S. OCS Regions

2011 Estimates

OCS Region	Undiscovered Economically Recoverable Resources (at a selected range of prices)	
	Oil (billion barrels)	Natural Gas (trillion cubic feet)
Alaska	1-22	1-85
Atlantic	1-2	8-18
Gulf of Mexico	33-45	130-198
Pacific	4-8	6-11

Source: Prepared by CRS; data from BOEM, *Assessment of Undiscovered Technically Recoverable Oil and Gas Resources of the Nation's Outer Continental Shelf*, 2011, Table 2 at http://www.boem.gov/uploadedFiles/2011_National_Assessment_Factsheet.pdf

Notes: The oil estimate is based on a price range of $30/barrel to $160/barrel. The natural gas estimate is based on a price range of $2.14/million cubic feet (Mcf) to $11.39/Mcf.

As interest in developing OCS resources in EPA's jurisdiction has increased, the EPA OCS air program has received increased scrutiny from some Members. In particular, Members have focused on the permit activity of Shell in the Chukchi Sea, part of the federal waters off Alaska's north coast. This interest led to the enactment of the Consolidated Appropriations Act, 2012 (P.L. 112-74) on December 23, 2011, which transferred air emission authority in the OCS off Alaska's north coast from the Environmental Protection Agency (EPA) to DOI.

This report will provide an overview and brief history of the separate regulatory programs, examine and compare the requirements of the programs, and highlight potential implications of the differences. Although OCS sources can involve other industry sectors (e.g., deepwater ports or offshore wind projects), the focus of this report is air emissions from the OCS oil and gas exploration, development, and production operations.

---

[9] For example, H.R. 2021 and H.R. 2055.

[10] For more information, see CRS Report R41153, *Changes in the Arctic: Background and Issues for Congress*, coordinated by Ronald O'Rourke.

Overview

OCS sources of air emissions can vary considerably, depending on the specifics of the operation. Offshore oil and gas sector operations, in particular, may include evolving technologies and take place in different settings, making it difficult to generalize air emission potentials. For example, mobile offshore drilling units involved in deepwater drilling in the Gulf of Mexico may emit considerably more emissions than a rig anchored to the sea floor in shallow water. Operations in the Arctic region may involve icebreaker vessels, which may generate considerably more emissions than other support vessels.

A Senate Report from the 1990 Clean Air Act (CAA) amendments stated: "The construction and operation of OCS facilities emit a significant amount of air pollution which adversely impacts coastal air quality in the United States. Operational emissions from an OCS platform and associated marine vessels can routinely exceed 500 tons of nitrogen (NO_x) and one hundred tons of reactive hydrocarbons annually."[11]

Based on a review of EPA OCS permit documents,[12] the 1990 Senate Report estimate is still valid, particularly for nitrogen oxide (NO_x) emissions. **Table 2** identifies emission ranges of selected air pollutants from seven OCS oil/gas operations seeking, or recently receiving, air permits in EPA's jurisdiction. In some cases, the ranges cover a wide spectrum. For each source, NO_x emissions account for the majority of the operations' regulated pollutants.

Four of the pollutants in **Table 2** are considered "criteria" pollutants and have a National Ambient Air Quality Standard (NAAQS).[13] Both NO_x and volatile organic carbon (VOC) emissions lead to ozone (O_3) formation (sometimes described as smog), which is also a criteria pollutant.

According to congressional testimony from EPA Administrator Jackson, "a single exploratory drilling operation could emit approximately as much air pollution on a daily basis as a large state-of-the-art oil refinery."[14]

---

[11] S. Rept. 101-228 (October 27, 1990).

[12] See permit materials (e.g., EPA's Statement of Basis documents) from EPA Region 4 and Region 10, at http://www.epa.gov/region4/air/permits/OCSPermits/OCSpermits.html and http://yosemite.epa.gov/R10/AIRPAGE.NSF/Permits/ocsap/. Accessed in September 2011.

[13] The CAA defines criteria pollutants as those that "endanger public health or welfare," and whose presence in ambient air "results from numerous or diverse mobile or stationary sources." Six pollutants are currently identified as such: ozone, particulates, carbon monoxide, sulfur dioxide, nitrogen oxides, and lead. See CRS Report R41563, *Clean Air Issues in the 112th Congress*, by James E. McCarthy.

[14] Lisa P. Jackson (EPA Administrator), Testimony before the House Committee on Oversight and Government Reform, May 24, 2011.

Table 2. Emission Ranges of Selected Air Pollutants from Outer Continental Shelf Oil/Gas Drilling Operations in EPA's Jurisdiction

(emissions in tons per year)

Carbon Monoxide (CO)	Nitrogen Oxides (NOₓ)	Particulate Matter (PM₁₀)	Sulfur Dioxide (SO₂)	Volatile Organic Compound (VOC)
60-855	443-2339	6-57	1-833	11-96

Source: Prepared by CRS; potentials to emit (PTE) from EPA Regions 4 and 10 permit documents, particularly the "Statement of Basis" documents, provided with each draft permit. Data supplying the above ranges are from nine OCS oil/gas drilling permits. See permit materials from EPA Regions 4 and 10, at http://www.epa.gov/region4/air/permits/ and http://yosemite.epa.gov/r10/airpage.nsf/permits/ocsap/. Accessed in November 2012.

Notes: The ranges are based on the operations' different potential to emit (PTE) values identified in the permit documents. Per 40 C.F.R. §52.21, PTE "means the maximum capacity of a stationary source to emit a pollutant under its physical and operational design. Any physical or operational limitation on the capacity of the source to emit a pollutant, including air pollution control equipment and restrictions on hours of operation or on the type or amount of material combusted, stored, or processed, shall be treated as part of its design if the limitation or the effect it would have on emissions is federally enforceable."

In several cases, EPA employed an air permit to require reductions from a pre-permitted PTE level, in order to avoid certain requirements (namely the PSD program, discussed below). The above ranges include the pre-permitted PTE values.

History of OCS Air Emission Governance

A brief history of federal OCS air emission governance may be instructive to policymakers. First, its history may help explain the rationale for the current framework. Second, some of the arguments made during its development may apply to current issues.

1953–1978

Passed as separate statutes in 1953, the Submerged Lands Act[15] and the Outer Continental Shelf Lands Act (OCSLA)[16] established federal jurisdiction and governance, respectively, for oil and gas resources on the OCS. The 1953 OCSLA did not specifically mention air emissions, but provided the Secretary of the Department of the Interior with general authority, stating: "The Secretary may at any time prescribe and amend such rules and regulations as he determines to be necessary and proper in order to provide for the prevention of waste and conservation of the natural resources of the outer Continental Shelf...."[17]

The Nixon Administration established the Environmental Protection Agency (EPA) in 1970 under an executive branch reorganization plan.[18] Although federal legislation addressing air pollution was first passed in 1955, the CAA Amendments of 1970 established the foundation of the federal

---

[15] May 22, 1953, 67 Stat. 29.

[16] August 7, 1953, 67 Stat. 464.

[17] 43 U.S.C. §1334 (from 1958 version).

[18] For more information, see CRS Report RL30798, *Environmental Laws: Summaries of Major Statutes Administered by the Environmental Protection Agency*, coordinated by David M. Bearden.

air emissions program that exists today.[19] For example, the 1970 law (among other provisions) set national standards for air quality, created a program to require the best available control technology at major new sources of air pollution, and established a program to regulate air toxics. In 1977, Congress made further amendments to the CAA, establishing (among other provisions) the prevention of significant deterioration (PSD) program.

Tension arose between the CAA provisions of the 1970s and the 1953 OCSLA. The 1953 OCSLA did not specifically mention which federal agency would have jurisdiction over the air quality effects of OCS development, resulting in uncertainty over what jurisdiction, if any, the newly created Environmental Protection Agency (EPA) had for air quality control in the OCS.[20] The jurisdictional uncertainty led EPA to assert its authority to regulate air emissions from OCS sources in April 1978.[21]

1978–1990

In September 1978, Congress passed the Outer Continental Shelf Lands Act of 1978 (P.L. 95-372),[22] providing the Department of the Interior (DOI) with authority to regulate the national offshore oil and gas program including the regulation of air emissions from offshore oil and gas operations.[23] A federal appeals court affirmed DOI's authority (versus EPA authority) in 1979, in a case brought by the State of California against DOI.[24] DOI issued regulations in 1980.

Some stakeholders in California continued to voice concerns regarding the level of control for OCS source air emissions. A 1992 report from the National Research Council stated:

> Offshore air pollution is a problem in California that is not present in other oil-producing regions in the country (with the possible exception of the West Coast of Florida). Atmospheric conditions peculiar to coastal California involve a combination of the amount of sunlight, the mixture of pollutants already present, the direction of prevailing winds, and the presence of coastal mountain ranges—all of which work to trap smog along the coastal strip. A major problem here has been that air quality standards for air above federal waters were not as stringent as those for state waters.[25]

---

[19] Congress made major amendments to the CAA in 1977 and 1990. See CRS Report RL30853, *Clean Air Act: A Summary of the Act and Its Major Requirements*, by James E. McCarthy et al.

[20] CRS Memorandum, Jurisdiction of OCS Air Quality Control in 1978 OCSLAA, September 23, 1988.

[21] 43 *Federal Register* 16393 (April 18, 1978).

[22] 43 U.S.C. §§1331-1356. The OCSLA was originally enacted in 1953, but has been amended several times.

[23] DOI delegated most of this responsibility to the Minerals Management Service. After the 2010 Deepwater Horizon incident the MMS was replaced by the Bureau of Ocean Energy Management, Regulation and Enforcement (BOEMRE), which was subsequently divided into two separate entities: the Bureau of Ocean Energy Management (BOEM) and the Bureau of Safety and Environmental Enforcement (BSEE).

[24] *California v. Kleppe*, 604 F.2d 1187 (9th Cir., 1979). For a discussion of this case, see Leon Harmon, "Recent Developments: *California v. Kleppe*" in *Environmental Law*, Vol. 10, No. 3, Spring 1980 (Northwestern School of Law of Lewis and Clark College).

[25] National Research Council, *Assessment of the U.S. Outer Continental Shelf Environmental Studies Program: Social and Economic Studies*, 1992, p. 129.

1990–Present

Congress made substantial amendments to the CAA in 1990.[26] A newly added Section 328 authorized EPA to implement certain air quality provisions of the act at offshore facilities, except for those west of 87.5 degrees longitude (i.e., Western and Central areas of the Gulf of Mexico). Offshore facilities not under EPA jurisdiction remain under DOI jurisdiction. EPA promulgated regulations for OCS sources in 1992.

In addition, Section 328(b) required the Secretary of the Interior to prepare a study assessing impacts of OCS sources in nonattainment areas that fail to meet NAAQS for ozone or nitrogen dioxide. Based on the results, the Secretary shall consult with the EPA Administrator to determine if additional actions are necessary. MMS published this study in 1995, which concluded that "the contribution of [OCS petroleum development] emission sources on onshore ozone concentrations is small."[27] The MMS regulations remained largely unchanged (discussed below).

Federal and State OCS Jurisdiction

The United States shares jurisdiction over its coastal waters with the coastal states. The 1953 Submerged Lands Act (SLA)[28] gave coastal states jurisdiction over the submerged lands, waters, and natural resources (e.g., oil deposits) located, in most cases, within 3 nautical miles off the coastline.[29] Within their offshore boundaries, coastal states have "(1) title to and ownership of the lands beneath navigable waters within the boundaries of the respective states, and (2) the right and power to manage, administer, lease, develop and use the said lands and natural resources...."[30] Accordingly, coastal states have the option of developing offshore oil and gas within their waters; if they choose to develop, they may regulate that development.

The waters, seabed, and natural resources beyond the states' waters are exclusively federal, and extend to the edge of the exclusive economic zone (200 nautical miles from shore).[31] However, the federal government maintains the authority to regulate commerce, navigation, national defense, power production, and international affairs within state waters.[32]

---

[26] Clean Air Act Amendments of 1990 (P.L. 101-549); 42 U.S.C. §7401 et seq.

[27] Minerals Management Service, *Gulf of Mexico Air Quality Study*, Final Report, Volume I, 1995, at http://www.gomr.boemre.gov/PI/PDFImages/ESPIS/3/3424.pdf.

[28] 43 U.S.C. §§1301-1315.

[29] Most state waters extend 3 nautical miles (1 nautical mile = 6,076 feet, or 1.15 miles) from shore. Louisiana waters extend 3 imperial nautical miles (1 imperial nautical mile = 6,080 feet). Texas and Gulf Coast of Florida waters extend 3 marine leagues (equating to 9 nautical miles). See CRS Report RL33404, *Offshore Oil and Gas Development: Legal Framework*, by Adam Vann.

[30] 43 U.S.C. §1311.

[31] The United States declared its EEZ in Presidential Proclamation No. 5030, 48 *Federal Register* 10605 (March 14, 1983). This declaration is consistent with the United Nations Convention on the Law of the Sea (UNCLOS). UNCLOS provides a comprehensive international legal framework intended for building consensus on actions related to the world's ocean spaces, uses, and resources. See United Nations Convention on the Law of the Sea, opened for signature December 10, 1982, in force November 16, 1994, 1833 U.N.T.S. 396, reprinted in United Nations, the Law of the Sea: United Nations Convention on the Law of the Sea (UN Pub. Sales No. E.83.V.5). For additional information, see CRS Report RS21890, *The U.N. Law of the Sea Convention and the United States: Developments Since October 2003*, by Marjorie Ann Browne.

[32] 43 U.S.C. §1314.

Role of OCS Moratoria

Decades long moratoria of oil and gas development for much of the OCS have influenced the level of interest regarding OCS air emission issues. As a result of public laws and executive orders of the President, OCS moratoria along the Atlantic and Pacific coasts, parts of Alaska, and the Gulf of Mexico have been in place since 1982. On July 14, 2008, President Bush lifted the executive moratoria, which included planning areas along the Atlantic and Pacific coasts. On September 30, 2008, moratoria provisions in annual appropriations laws expired, allowing these areas to potentially open for oil and gas leasing activity.[33]

Thus, most of the OCS in EPA's jurisdiction has been off limits to oil and gas development until recently. Moreover, once a moratorium is removed, multiple legal and administrative processes must be satisfied before actual drilling can occur in a particular area.[34]

EPA OCS Air Program

CAA Section 328 provides the underlying authority for EPA's OCS program. Pursuant to this section, EPA established two regulatory regimes: one for OCS sources located within 25 miles of a state's seaward boundary ("inner OCS sources");[35] another for OCS sources located beyond 25 miles of a state's water boundary and extending to the boundary of the EEZ ("outer OCS sources").

EPA created the separate regimes based on the text of Section 328. This section directs EPA to develop regulations requiring all OCS sources "to attain and maintain Federal and State ambient air quality standards and to comply with the provisions of [the prevention of significant deterioration (PSD) program]."[36] In addition, Section 328 creates a more comprehensive program for inner sources, stating: "**Such requirements shall be the same as would be applicable if the source were located in the corresponding onshore area**, and shall include, but not be limited to, State and local requirements for emission controls, emission limitations, offsets, permitting, monitoring, testing, and reporting [emphasis added]."

EPA promulgated regulations—40 C.F.R. Part 55—in 1992 for OCS source air emissions.[37] Selected elements of these regulations are discussed below. In several instances, Part 55 directs OCS sources to air emission regulations in other CAA regulations, codified in separate parts of the *Code of Federal Regulations*. In general, these cross-references include the most substantive requirements for OCS sources.

---

[33] For more information, see CRS Report R41132, *Outer Continental Shelf Moratoria on Oil and Gas Development*, by Curry L. Hagerty.

[34] See CRS Report RL33404, *Offshore Oil and Gas Development: Legal Framework*, by Adam Vann.

[35] Most state waters extend 3 nautical miles (1 nautical mile = 6,076 feet, or 1.15 miles) from shore. Florida is the only state within EPA's jurisdiction with a different boundary: the Gulf Coast of Florida waters extend 3 marine leagues (equating to 9 nautical miles). See also CRS Report RL33404, *Offshore Oil and Gas Development: Legal Framework*, by Adam Vann. See the BOEMRE OCS website ("Definitions and Information") at http://boemre.gov/incidents/def_info.htm.

[36] 42 U.S.C. §7627.

[37] 57 *Federal Register* 40792 (September 4, 1992).

Outer OCS Source Requirements

Compared to inner OCS source requirements, outer OCS source requirements are fewer and *relatively* less complex, because sources need only comply with federal regulations. EPA argued in its rulemaking proposal that CAA Section 328 gave the agency "some latitude" to determine the regulations for outer sources.[38] In addition to PSD requirements (which Section 328 specifically identified), EPA chose to apply New Source Performance Standards (NSPS), National Emission Standards for Hazardous Air Pollutants (NESHAPS), and CAA Title V permitting provisions to outer OCS sources. These are discussed below.

Prevention of Significant Deterioration

Pursuant to CAA Section 328 (and 40 C.F.R. Part 55) OCS sources are potentially subject to the CAA's Prevention of Significant Deterioration (PSD) program. Congress added the PSD program to the CAA in 1977[39] to address new or modified emission sources that would affect areas meeting National Ambient Air Quality Standards (NAAQS).[40] The primary objective of the program is to ensure that the air quality does not degrade in these areas with the addition of a new (or modified) source.

An OCS source that qualifies as a "major stationary source"[41] must comply with PSD provisions. The primary determinant is an annual emissions threshold. For any stationary source, the threshold is 250 tons per year (tpy) of a regulated pollutant.[42] Some specific emission sources have a lower threshold of 100 tpy. Oil and gas exploration, development, and production activities are not among these specific sources.[43] Regardless, many OCS sources from the oil/gas industry are likely to approach or breach the 250 tpy threshold (**Table 2**).

In addition to the 250 tpy threshold, as of January 2, 2011, an OCS source must consider its greenhouse gas (GHG) emissions.[44] These emissions are subject to a different threshold. Per a 2010 rulemaking, EPA is phasing in GHG applicability for the PSD program.[45] As of July 1, 2011 (the start of the second of four phases), new emission sources—not already subject to PSD for other pollutants—would be subject to PSD, if GHG emissions equal or exceed 100,000 tpy of

---

[38] 56 *Federal Register* 63774 (December 5, 1991).

[39] CAA §§160-169.

[40] Such areas are termed "attainment areas." For more information, see CRS Report RL30853, *Clean Air Act: A Summary of the Act and Its Major Requirements*, by James E. McCarthy et al.

[41] 40 C.F.R. §52.21(b). In the CAA, the applicable term is "major emitting facility" (CAA §169).

[42] The official term is "regulated NSR [New Source Review] pollutant," which includes (among others) any pollutant for which a national ambient air quality standard (NAAQS) has been promulgated—sulfur dioxide (SO_2), particulate matter ($PM_{2.5}$ and PM_{10}), nitrogen dioxide (NO_2), carbon monoxide (CO), ozone, and lead—and any pollutant identified (in this citation) as a constituent or precursor for a regulated NSR pollutant (40 C.F.R. §52.21(b)(50)).

[43] CAA §169(1) lists 28 categories of sources with the 100 tpy threshold (also in 40 C.F.R. §52.21(b)). These sources include specific industries, such as cement plants and petroleum refineries, but not oil/gas exploration, development, or production activities.

[44] In the context of the PSD program, GHGs are the aggregate group of the following six gases: carbon dioxide (CO_2) nitrous oxide (N_2O), methane (CH_4), hydrofluorocarbons, perfluorocarbons, and sulfur hexafluoride (SF_6) (40 C.F.R. §52.21(b)(49)).

[45] For more information, see CRS Report R41212, *EPA Regulation of Greenhouse Gases: Congressional Responses and Options*, by James E. McCarthy.

---

carbon dioxide equivalents (CO_2e).[46] If an OCS source is already subject to PSD for one or more of the 250 tpy-threshold pollutants, the GHG emission threshold is 75,000 tpy of CO_2e.[47]

If an OCS source meets the definition of a "major stationary source," several PSD requirements apply. Selected requirements are discussed below, followed by an exemption for certain OCS sources.

Best Available Control Technology (BACT)

A source must apply BACT for each regulated pollutant that would be emitted in significant amounts.[48] This means that a source may qualify as a "major stationary source" based on only one pollutant, but may need BACT for multiple pollutants.[49] The significant amounts for selected pollutants are listed in **Table 3**.

Table 3. Selected Significant Emission Rates in PSD Program

(tons per year)

CO	NO$_x$	SO$_2$	PM	PM$_{10}$	PM$_{2.5}$	Ozone
100	40	40	25	15	10[a]	40[b]

Source: 40 C.F.R. §52.21(b)(23).

a. 10 tpy of direct PM$_{2.5}$ emissions; 40 tpy of SO$_2$ emissions; 40 tpy of NO$_x$ emissions unless demonstrated not to be a PM2.5 precursor.

b. 40 tpy of VOC compounds or NO$_x$.

BACT is determined on a case-by-case basis, taking into account a proposed control measure's energy, environmental, and economic impacts.[50] Most states have the authority to implement the PSD program and set BACT for applicable sources, but as mentioned above, only a handful of locales have Part 55 (OCS regulatory) authority. Therefore, the applicable EPA Region would determine BACT for OCS sources in most locations.[51] Due to the moratoria, EPA has made such determinations in only a few instances.

---

[46] GHG emissions are often presented in carbon dioxide equivalents (CO_2e), because GHGs vary by global warming potential (GWP). GWP is an index of how much a GHG may contribute to global warming over a period of time, typically 100 years. GWPs are used to compare gases to CO_2, which has a GWP of 1. For example, methane's GWP is 25, and thus a ton of methane is 25 times more potent a GHG than a ton of CO_2.

[47] For more information, see U.S. EPA, "Prevention of Significant Deterioration and Title V Greenhouse Gas Tailoring Rule," 75 *Federal Register* 31514. A six-page EPA Fact Sheet summarizing the rule is available at http://www.epa.gov/nsr/documents/20100413fs.pdf.

[48] 40 C.F.R. §52.21(j).

[49] The regulations list the "significant amounts" for each pollutant in 40 C.F.R. §52.21(b)(23).

[50] 40 C.F.R. §52.21(b)(12).

[51] For more information, see EPA Region 4, *Prevention of Significant Deterioration Permit Application Requirements,* (updated February 2010), which references EPA, *New Source Review Workshop Manual-Prevention of Significant Deterioration and Nonattainment Area Permitting*, Draft Guidance, 1990.

Air Quality Demonstration and Analyses

A source must demonstrate that its emissions would not cause or contribute significantly to a violation of the NAAQS[52] or any allowable maximum increase over the baseline concentration.[53] To meet this demonstration, a source must provide an air quality analysis for each pollutant it would emit in a significant amount.[54] In general, the pollutant analysis must include at least one year of continuous air quality monitoring data.[55]

A source must provide further analysis regarding impacts to visibility and soils and vegetation.[56] If a source's emissions may impact a Class I area—156 listed national memorials, monuments, parks, and wilderness over certain sizes—[57] EPA must consult with the applicable Federal Land Manager. The Manager has the opportunity to demonstrate that the source would yield adverse impacts, such as reduced visibility. If EPA accepts this demonstration, the source would not receive a permit. If EPA disagrees, the agency must provide a publicly available explanation.[58]

Emissions Monitoring and Reporting

Pursuant to PSD regulatory authority, EPA may require a source to continue to monitor ambient air emissions during its operation to determine the effect of the emissions.[59] EPA may exempt a source from this requirement, if a source's emission levels are below pollutant-specific thresholds.[60] Part 55 also contains provisions authorizing EPA to require emissions monitoring.[61]

Exemption for Temporary Sources

OCS exploratory drilling operations may qualify for an exemption from certain PSD program requirements. The exemption has two conditions. First, regulated emissions from the major stationary source must not impact a Class I area (discussed above). Second, the source's emissions must be "temporary."[62] EPA has not defined "temporary" in the PSD regulations, but in a 1980 *Federal Register* preamble, EPA stated that it considered sources operating for less than two years in a given location to be temporary sources.[63]

Sources meeting the conditions of the exemption are not subject to the air quality demonstration and analyses discussed above. Several of OCS exploratory drilling operations that received EPA air permits qualified as temporary sources.

---

[52] For more information on NAAQS, see CRS Report RL30853, *Clean Air Act: A Summary of the Act and Its Major Requirements*, by James E. McCarthy et al.

[53] 40 C.F.R. §52.21(k).

[54] 40 C.F.R. §52.21(m).

[55] EPA has the discretion to shorten this time frame to a period not less than four months (40 C.F.R. §52.21(m)).

[56] 40 C.F.R. §52.21(o).

[57] 40 C.F.R. §52.21(e).

[58] 40 C.F.R. §52.21(p).

[59] 40 C.F.R. §52.21(m)(2).

[60] 40 C.F.R. §52.21(i)(5).

[61] 40 C.F.R. §55.8.

[62] 40 C.F.R. §52.21(i)(3).

[63] 45 *Federal Register* 52676 (August 7, 1980).

New Source Performance Standards

Part 55 requires OCS sources to comply with applicable New Source Performance Standards (NSPS) in 40 C.F.R. Part 60. NSPS are nationally uniform, technology-based standards for specific categories of stationary emission sources.[64] The format of the standard can vary from source to source, and may entail a numerical emission limit, a design standard, an equipment standard, or a work practice standard.

Offshore oil development operations may involve equipment that has a NSPS. For example, several OCS draft permits prepared by EPA identify specific internal combustion engines with a NSPS in 40 C.F.R. Part 60, Subpart IIII.[65]

National Emission Standards for Hazardous Air Pollutants

OCS sources may be subject to National Emission Standards for Hazardous Air Pollutants (NESHAP). Part 55 requires compliance with any regulations promulgated pursuant to CAA Section 112,[66] if they are "rationally related to the attainment and maintenance of Federal or State ambient air quality standards or the requirements of [the PSD program]."[67]

EPA has promulgated multiple regulations pursuant to CAA Section 112 (e.g., 40 C.F.R. Parts 61 and 63). In general, these regulations establish emissions standards for hazardous air pollutants released from specific sources (e.g., industries or equipment). Whether these regulations apply depends on the operating equipment of the specific OCS source.

Based on OCS permit documents from EPA Region 4 and Region 10, existing provisions in Part 61 are unlikely to apply to an OCS oil/gas drilling operation.[68] Several of the permits identify equipment that would be potentially subject to provisions in Part 63 (e.g., Subpart ZZZZ, which regulates reciprocating internal combustion engines). However, in many cases the units satisfy Subpart ZZZZ requirements by complying with the NSPS in 40 C.F.R. Part 60, Subpart IIII (mentioned above).

Title V/Part 71 Operating Permits

A source may require a Title V permit, but not be subject to the provisions of other parts of the CAA, such as BACT under the PSD program. The emissions threshold for a regulated pollutant is lower for Title V than the PSD program. Instead of 250 tpy (as discussed above), the Title V threshold is generally 100 tpy.[69]

---

[64] As technology evolves, EPA adds new standards (per CAA §111). 40 C.F.R. Part 60 contains over 90 standards.

[65] See e.g., EPA Region 4, Draft Permit to Shell Offshore Inc., at http://www.epa.gov/region4/air/permits/OCSPermits/OCSpermits.html

[66] For further discussion of CAA Section 112, see CRS Report RL30853, *Clean Air Act: A Summary of the Act and Its Major Requirements*, by James E. McCarthy et al.

[67] 40 C.F.R. §55.13(e).

[68] Although several permit documents identify Part 61, Subpart J (fugitive benzene emissions from specific equipment) as potentially applicable, none of the operations were ultimately subject to Part 61. See "Statement of Basis" documents from EPA Region 4 and Region 10, at http://www.epa.gov/region4/air/permits/OCSPermits/OCSpermits.html and http://yosemite.epa.gov/R10/AIRPAGE.NSF/Permits/ocsap/. Accessed in September 2011.

[69] CAA Title V, which references CAA Section 302 and the definition of "major stationary source." This is codified in (continued...)

Part 55 directs outer OCS sources to 40 C.F.R. Part 71, which contains the regulations promulgated to CAA Title V. The primary purpose of the Title V permit program is administrative/enforcement efficiency. Title V permits collect all applicable requirements in a single permit. Title V permits are not intended to change or alter the existing, underlying requirements or add requirements.[70]

Although some may describe the Title V permit provisions as non-substantive, others may view them as onerous. Title V permits are issued for five-year periods and must be renewed thereafter. Permits generally require the following:

- emissions limitations and standards to assure compliance with all applicable requirements;

- emissions monitoring, recordkeeping, and reporting;

- fee payments to support administrative expenses; and

- annual certification by a responsible official of the source.

Inner OCS Source Requirements

Inner OCS sources are subject to all of the requirements for outer OCS sources (described above) and any applicable state and/or local air emissions requirements. In the event of conflict between federal and state/local regulations, the more stringent provisions would apply.[71]

Attainment vs. Nonattainment Areas

Compared to outer OCS sources, the location of the inner OCS source plays a key role in determining its applicable emission requirements. This is a function of the CAA and the potential variety of regulations among states and locales. A fundamental element of the CAA, which is generally implemented by states (at least for onshore sources), is its approach of setting more stringent standards for areas not meeting certain air quality standards ("nonattainment areas").[72] For example, in a nonattainment area, an inner OCS source may be subject to the lowest achievable emission rate (LAER), which is by definition more stringent than BACT.[73] In addition, emissions from new or modified sources must also be offset by reductions in emissions from existing sources.

For the OCS air permits recently issued by EPA—in the eastern Gulf of Mexico and off the northern Coast of Alaska (Beaufort and Chukchi Seas)—the nearby coastal areas are in

---

(...continued)

40 C.F.R. part 71. The threshold for hazardous air pollutants is even lower: 10 tpy of an individual hazardous pollutant or more than 25 tpy of any combination.

[70] For more information, see CRS Report RL33632, *Clean Air Permitting: Implementation and Issues*, by Claudia Copeland.

[71] C.F.R. §55.14.

[72] For more information, see CRS Report RL30853, *Clean Air Act: A Summary of the Act and Its Major Requirements*, by James E. McCarthy et al. See also,

[73] As mentioned above, a BACT determination may consider a proposed control measure's energy, environmental, and economic impacts.

---

attainment.[74] In general, the coastal non-attainment areas for pollutants common to OCS oil/gas operations (e.g., ozone) are located in California and the Mid Atlantic (**Figure 2**).[75] If OCS operations expand, nonattainment areas may become more of a factor.[76]

Figure 2. Map of Non-Attainment Areas for Ozone (8-Hour)

Based on 1997 Standard

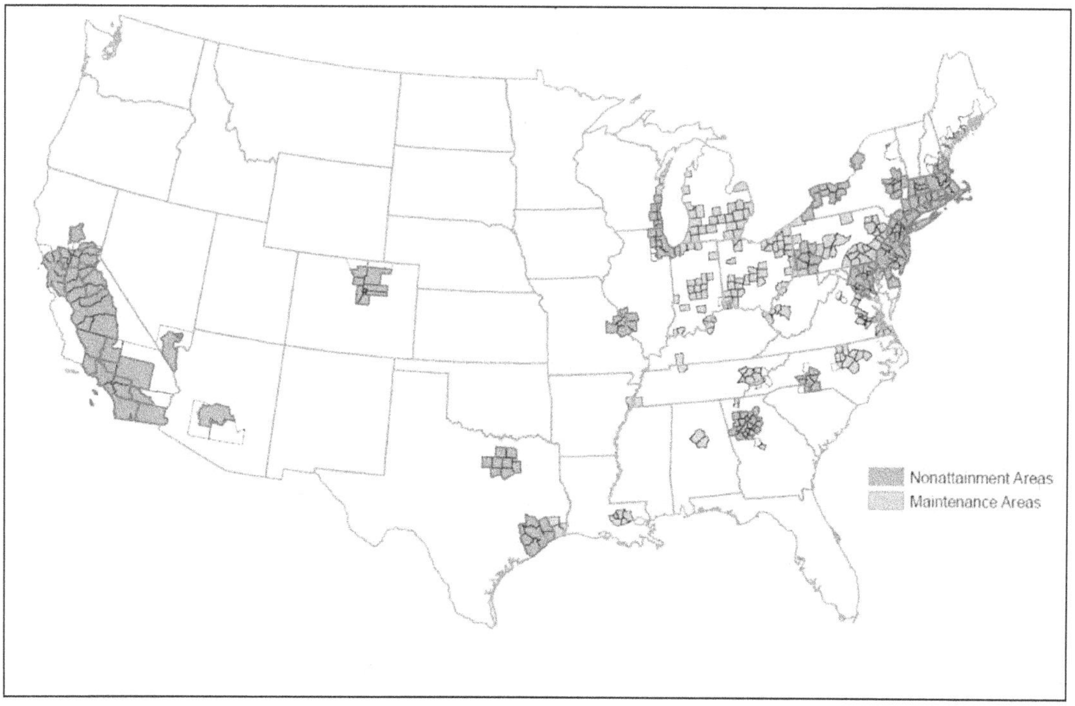

Source: Reproduced from EPA Office of Air and Radiation, at http://www.epa.gov/airquality/greenbook/map/map8hrnm.pdf (accessed November 26, 2012).

Note: EPA's nonattainment map for ozone is based on its 1997 ozone NAAQ, which was lowered from 0.08 parts per million (ppm) to 0.075 ppm in 2008. See CRS Report R41563, *Clean Air Issues in the 112th Congress*, by James E. McCarthy.

---

[74] Although P.L. 112-74 (signed by President Obama December 23, 2011) transferred air emission authority in the OCS off Alaska's north coast to DOI, the act states the transfer "shall not invalidate or stay (1) any air quality permit pending or existing as of the date of the enactment of this Act; or (2) any proceeding related thereto" (Section 432).

[75] Of the recently EPA-issued OCS air permits, nitrogen oxide (NO_x) emissions were the primary reason an OCS source required a permit. Although the United States has no nitrogen dioxide (NO_2) non-attainment areas (per EPA's Office of Air and Radiation website, at http://www.epa.gov/air), NO_x emissions are precursors for ozone and $PM_{2.5}$.

[76] EPA's nonattainment map for ozone (**Error! Reference source not found.**) is based on its 1997 ozone NAAQS. EPA lowered this standard from 0.08 parts per million (ppm) to 0.075 ppm in 2008, but nonattainment areas for the new standard have not yet been designated. In addition, EPA proposed a further reduced standard (in the range of 0.06 – 0.07 ppm) on January 19, 2010 (75 *Federal Register* 2938). EPA withdrew this proposal in September 2011. According to EPA's estimate, the proposed standard would have increased the number of non-attainment counties from 85 to 515. For more information, see CRS Report R41563, *Clean Air Issues in the 112th Congress*, by James E. McCarthy.

Notice of Intent/Corresponding Onshore Area Designation

An owner/operator of an inner OCS source must submit a Notice of Intent (NOI) to the appropriate EPA regional office and the appropriate state agency (or agencies) of the nearest onshore area and adjacent areas. Among other elements, the NOI must include (1) an estimate of the source's potential emissions (in tons per year) of any air pollutant; and (2) information allowing for an analysis of the source's impact in onshore areas.[77] As discussed below, the NOI must include emission information from vessels associated with the operation.

The main purpose of the NOI is to allow the applicable state agency to decide if it wants to submit a request as corresponding onshore area (COA).[78] The CAA requires OCS sources to comply with air emission provisions applicable to onshore sources in the COA. In general, the onshore area closest to the OCS source is considered the COA. The act provides EPA with the authority to designate another area as the COA, if that area has more stringent air emission controls and that area will be impacted by emissions from the OCS source.[79] For this to occur, the state agency from the state seeking a COA redesignation must make a formal request to EPA. EPA must make a COA designation determination—based on state agency documentation and following a public comment period—within 240 days of receiving the NOI from the OCS source.

EPA regulations do not allow a COA redesignation for exploratory OCS sources (e.g., exploratory drilling operations). The statute is silent on this issue, but EPA determined it was unreasonable to require an exploratory source, which (according to EPA) may operate for 3-4 months, to undergo an administrative procedure that can last for 8 months.[80]

OCS Vessel Emissions

Air emissions from vessels associated with OCS operations have generated some interest and debate.[81] In some offshore oil and gas operations, the emissions from vessels may represent a substantial percentage of the operation's overall air emissions. Section 328(a)(4)(C) states:

> The terms "Outer Continental Shelf source" and "OCS source" include any equipment, activity, or facility which—
>
> (i) emits or has the potential to emit any air pollutant,
>
> (ii) is regulated or authorized under the Outer Continental Shelf Lands Act [43 U.S.C. 1331 et seq.], and
>
> (iii) is located on the Outer Continental Shelf or in or on waters above the Outer Continental Shelf.

---

[77] 40 C.F.R. §55.4

[78] 40 C.F.R. §55.5.

[79] CAA §328(a)(4)(B), 42 U.S.C. 7627(a)(4)(B).

[80] 57 *Federal Register* 40795 (September 4, 1992).

[81] Some raised the issue again during Shell's air permit process for drilling in the Chukchi Sea. See EPA Environmental Appeals Board, Opinion Regarding Shell OCS Permit, Decided December 30, 2010.

Such activities include, but are not limited to, platform and drill ship exploration, construction, development, production, processing, and transportation. For purposes of this subsection, emissions from any vessel servicing or associated with an OCS source, including emissions while at the OCS source or en route to or from the OCS source within 25 miles of the OCS source, shall be considered direct emissions from the OCS source.[82]

While crafting the regulations (40 C.F.R. Part 55) implementing CAA Section 328, EPA interpreted the above provision to include vessels as OCS sources only when (1) they are permanently or temporarily attached to the seabed for the purpose of exploring, producing, or developing natural resource activities; or (2) they are physically attached to an OCS facility.[83] If a vessel qualifies as an OCS source, it may need to comply with other sections of the CAA, namely the PSD program and BACT.

Emissions from support vessels (i.e., non-OCS source vessels) play a role in how the OCS source the vessels support is regulated. All air emissions, including transit-related emissions within 25 miles of the OCS source, from support vessels must be accounted for in an OCS source's "potential to emit." In some situations, the support vessel emissions may cause the OCS source's emissions to cross regulatory thresholds (i.e., 250 tpy of regulated pollutants in the case of PSD).[84]

State Authority

Coastal states may seek authority to implement and enforce air emission requirements for OCS sources in federal waters adjacent to state waters.[85] This authority can include sources within the 25 mile seaward boundary and/or sources beyond this boundary.[86] To obtain this authority, a governor must submit his/her state regulations to the EPA Administrator, who determines if the state provisions are adequate, based on specific criteria.[87] If a state does not seek delegation, EPA implements the program in waters adjacent to that state. In addition, if a neighboring state has sought and received a COA redesignation (as discussed above), EPA may implement the more stringent standards of this neighboring state.[88]

---

[82] 42 U.S.C. §7627(a)(4)(C).

[83] 57 *Federal Register* 40792 (September 4, 1992). EPA's rationale for this interpretation relates to the second clause in the OCS definition: "is regulated or authorized under the [OCSLA]." According to EPA, the OCSLA (43 U.S.C. 1333) specifically excludes ships and vessels (unless permanently or temporarily attached to the seabed) from its regulatory authority.

[84] For example, see EPA permit (and associated documents) for Shell for oil exploration in the Chukchi Sea (issued September 19, 2011), at http://yosemite.epa.gov/R10/airpage.nsf/Permits/chukchiap/.

[85] CAA §328(a)(3).

[86] 40 C.F.R. §55.11(a). This latter authority was not included in the initial final rule, but added by a subsequent rulemaking (62 *Federal Register* 46406, September 2, 1997).

[87] 40 C.F.R. §55.11(b).

[88] Provided in 40 C.F.R. §55.11(j).

According to a 2008 EPA *Federal Register* notice, only four local air pollution control agencies in California[89] have received authority to implement Part 55.[90] This relatively small number is likely related to the moratoria. EPA implements and enforces the regulations for all other sources within EPA's jurisdiction, including the state/local air emission regulations for inner OCS sources. If policymakers open more OCS areas to oil/gas activities, this dynamic may change.

Procedural Requirements

Although Part 55 does not include specific administrative procedures and public participation requirements, statutory provisions and requirements referenced in Part 55 would apply. **Table 4** identifies procedural time frames for PSD and Title V permits that would apply to outer OCS sources. Inner OCS sources would be subject to the same standards as onshore sources. These standards vary by state and may be more stringent than the time frames identified below.

Table 4. EPA Review of PSD and Title V Permits

(outer OCS sources)

Time Frames	PSD Permit	Title V Permit[a]
For EPA to review permit to determine if application is complete	30 days[b]	Deemed complete within 60 days of receipt, unless EPA determines otherwise within that time frame[c]
After deemed submitted, public comment period	30 days (with extension at EPA's discretion)[d]	30 days (with extension at EPA's discretion)[e]
Final Decision	I year after filing of completed permit application[f]	18 months after receiving a completed permit application[g]

Source: Prepared by CRS.

Note: Inner OCS sources would be subject to state/local air emission requirements, which may include more stringent time frames than identified above.

a. OCS sources can apply for a Title V permit within 12 months after first becoming a source (40 C.F.R. §71.5).

b. 40 C.F.R. §124.3.

c. 40 C.F.R. §71.5

d. 40 C.F.R. §124.10

e. 40 C.F.R. §71.11.

f. 42 U.S.C. §7475(c).

g. 40 C.F.R. §71.7.

[89] Santa Barbara County Air Pollution Control District (SBCAPCD); South Coast Air Quality Management District (SCAQMD); Ventura County Air Pollution Control District (VCAPCD); and San Luis Obispo County Air Pollution Control District (SLOAPCD).

[90] 73 *Federal Register* 66037 (November 8, 2008).

Public Participation

In general, when EPA prepares a draft permit, the agency must provide 30 days for public comment.[91] Parties may request a public hearing,[92] which EPA must hold if the Administrator "finds, on the basis of requests, a significant degree of public interest in a draft permit."[93] In addition, the agency has the discretion to extend the comment period beyond 30 days,[94] and it may reopen the comment period to expedite the decision process.[95]

Administrative Appeals Process

PSD and Title V permits are subject to an administrative appeals process. Any person who submitted comments concerning the draft permit (or participated in a public hearing) may petition—within 30 days of the final permit decision—EPA's Environmental Appeals Board (EAB) to review any condition of the permit.[96] In addition, the EAB may decide on its own initiative to review conditions in a permit. The EAB must issue its decision "within a reasonable time" after receiving a petition.[97]

Judicial Review

In addition, parties may contest EPA's permit decision in the court system. Judicial review of permit decisions is typically governed by the particular environmental statute that is the subject of the litigation.[98] CAA Section 307 provides for judicial review of EPA actions. In addition, CAA Section 502 includes judicial review provisions for Title V permit activity, providing an opportunity for judicial review in state court of final permit actions by the applicant, persons who participated in the public comment process, and any other person who could obtain judicial review of such actions under state laws.[99] However, parties must go through the EAB process before seeking judicial review of agency action.[100]

---

[91] 40 C.F.R. §124.10; 40 C.F.R. §71.11.

[92] 40 C.F.R. §124.11; 40 C.F.R. §71.11.

[93] 40 C.F.R. §124.12; 40 C.F.R. §71.11.

[94] 40 C.F.R. §124.13; 40 C.F.R. §71.11.

[95] 40 C.F.R. §124.14; 40 C.F.R. §71.11.

[96] 40 C.F.R. §124.19; 40 C.F.R. §71.11.

[97] Further information regarding the EAB is available at http://www.epa.gov/eab/.

[98] If a specific statute is silent, the Administrative Procedures Act provides for judicial review. For more information, see CRS Report R41546, *A Brief Overview of Rulemaking and Judicial Review*, by Todd Garvey and Daniel T. Shedd.

[99] See CRS Report RL33632, *Clean Air Permitting: Implementation and Issues*, by Claudia Copeland.

[100] "A petition to the Environmental Appeals Board under paragraph (a) of this section is, under 5 U.S.C. 704, a prerequisite to the seeking of judicial review of the final agency action" (40 C.F.R. 124.19(e)). For further information, see EPA, *The Environmental Appeals Board: Practice Manual*, September 2010.

DOI OCS Air Program

The DOI authority to address OCS air emissions comes from the 1978 OCSLA, which directs the DOI Secretary to promulgate regulations "for compliance with the national ambient air quality standards pursuant to the Clean Air Act (42 U.S.C. 7401 et seq.), to the extent that activities authorized under this subchapter significantly affect the air quality of any State."[101]

To satisfy this directive, DOI (acting through the U.S. Geological Survey) promulgated regulations in 1980.[102] The regulations were redesignated (i.e., renumbered) in 1998,[103] but the 1980 provisions generally remain the same in 2011. The recent administrative changes (described in the earlier "Reader's Note") have led to a further restructuring of the regulations. An October 2011 direct final rule separated BOEM and BSEE regulations, creating 30 C.F.R. Part 550 for BOEM provisions (BSEE regulations were retained in their original location).[104] The rule did not add or remove OCS requirements, but makes organizational changes needed to accommodate the DOI administrative changes.

In addition, DOI or its agencies (e.g., MMS, BOEM) have periodically issued Notices to Lessees and Operators (NTLs), which "clarify, supplement, or provide more detail about certain requirements."[105]

Activity-Specific Plan Requirements

Before conducting operations on the OCS, leaseholders must (among other requirements) submit and receive approval for activity-specific plans. For example, the OCSLA requires lessees to have an approved Exploration Plan (EP) for exploration activities[106] and a Development and Production Plan (DPP) for development and production activities[107] or a Development Operations Coordination Document (DOCC) in areas, such as portions of the Western Gulf of Mexico, where significant activities have already taken place.[108] (Hereafter in this report, references to DPPs include DOCCs.) BOEM is charged with reviewing and approving these plans.[109]

These plans must include, among other provisions, a facility's projected emissions (in tpy and other measurements) of SO_2, particulate matter (measured in $PM_{2.5}$ and PM_{10} when applicable), NO_x, CO, and volatile organic compounds (VOC).[110] The lessee will apply these projections, and other related information (e.g., distance from shore), to determine whether certain requirements apply (e.g., BACT).

---

[101] 43 U.S.C. §1334(a)(8).

[102] 45 *Federal Register* 15128 (March 7, 1980).

[103] 63 *Federal Register* 29487 (May 29, 1998).

[104] 76 *Federal Register* 64432 (October 18, 2011).

[105] 30 C.F.R. §250.103 (BSEE) and §550.103 (BOEM).

[106] 43 U.S.C. §1340.

[107] 43 U.S.C. §1351.

[108] 30 C.F.R. §250.201 (BSEE) and §550.201 (BOEM).

[109] BSEE reviews Deepwater Operations Plans (DWOPs), but these are supplemental to other activity-specific plans and do not have additional air emission provisions.

[110] 30 C.F.R. §550.218 (EP) or §550.249 (DPP or DOCC).

A 2009 NTL stated that these requirements apply "regardless of whether the proposed activities are in an area under [DOI] jurisdiction or EPA air quality jurisdiction."[111]

Exemption Determination

A primary determination is whether the OCS source is exempt from further air emission requirements. The DOI regulations contain an exemption formula, based on projected emissions and distance from shore.[112] For all of the pollutants listed above except CO emissions, the exemption formula is:

$$E = 33.3D$$

Where:

E equals the exemption threshold (in tpy), and

D equals distance from shore (in miles).

For example, if an OCS source would be located 30 miles from shore, it would be exempt from further air emission requirements as long as the projected emissions for each pollutant (SO_2, PM, NO_x, and VOC) were below its exemption threshold of 990 tpy.[113] Note the primary threshold for EPA's substantive requirements (e.g., PSD program) is 250 tpy, and states may have even lower thresholds that would apply to inner OCS sources.

Significance Determination

For a non-exempt OCS source, the next determination is whether projected air emissions from any pollutants would "significantly" affect onshore air quality (VOC emissions from non-exempt sources are automatically deemed to significantly affect onshore air quality). These sources must make the significance determination by using an approved air quality model.[114] If the model indicates that air pollutant concentrations—specified in 40 C.F.R. §550.303(e)—would be exceeded, the facility's emissions would significantly affect onshore air quality. The DOI significance levels are the same required by EPA when determining whether a new major source would significantly impact the air quality of a neighboring nonattainment area.[115]

Required Emission Controls

If air emissions from a non-exempt OCS source would significantly affect the air quality of an onshore area (based on the modeling described above), further requirements apply. The requirements depend on whether the impacted onshore location is an attainment (or

---

[111] MMS NTL No. 2009-N11, "Air Quality Jurisdiction on the OCS," effective December 4, 2009.

[112] 30 C.F.R. §550.303(d).

[113] The CO emission exemption formula is $E = 3400D^{2/3}$. Thus, a facility 50 miles from shore would be exempt if its projected CO emissions were less than 46,750 tpy.

[114] 30 C.F.R. §550.303(e).

[115] EPA levels are in 40 C.F.R. §51.165(b).

unclassifiable) or nonattainment area. If more than one area would be impacted, the more stringent requirements would apply.[116]

Emissions Monitoring and Reporting

According to the DOI regulations, lessees must monitor air emissions ("in a manner approved or prescribed by the Regional Supervisor") regardless of the source's exempt status or whether the OCS source's emissions would significantly impact air quality.[117] In addition, the regulations require lessees to submit emission information to DOI on a monthly basis. However, it is uncertain whether OCS sources are complying with this provision as written.

Nonattainment Areas

For nonattainment areas (e.g., **Figure 2**), the source must "fully reduce" emissions of any pollutant that would significantly affect air quality. To achieve this objective, the lessee must apply BACT, which, like EPA's definition, allows for the consideration of energy, environmental, and economic impacts. The lessee determines BACT, but a regional BOEM official verifies BACT on a case-by-case basis.[118]

By comparison, EPA imposes LAER for new (inner OCS) sources in nonattainment areas, a potentially more stringent control. However, if BACT alone would not address the applicable emissions at an OCS source in DOI's jurisdiction, the source must make additional reductions or acquire emission offsets from another source.[119]

Attainment Areas

If attainment areas would be affected, an OCS source must apply BACT to emissions of any air pollutant that would significantly affect air quality in the attainment area. In addition, the lessee must determine whether—after applying BACT—emissions of total suspended particulates (TSP) or SO_2 would increase emission concentrations over specified thresholds ("maximum allowable increases") in the applicable area.[120] The specified maximum allowable increases are similar to those in EPA's PSD regulations.[121] However, the EPA regulations address PM_{10} instead of TSP emissions, and also include NO_2 emissions. The likely explanation for this difference is that the DOI regulations reflect the EPA standards in place in 1980. Since that time, EPA has revised standards and added new pollutants.[122]

---

[116] 30 C.F.R. §550.303(g)(4).

[117] 30 C.F.R. §550.303(k).

[118] 30 C.F.R. §550.302. See also the 1980 *Federal Register* preamble that states: "The Department also believes that it is appropriate, particularly in the initial stages, for lessees to identify BACT." 45 Federal Register 15135 (March 7, 1980).

[119] 30 C.F.R. §550.303(g).

[120] 30 C.F.R. §550.303(g).

[121] 40 C.F.R. §52.21(c).

[122] For example, EPA replaced the TSP standard with the PM_{10} standard in 1987 (52 *Federal Register* 24634, July 1, 1987). See also http://www.epa.gov/pm/history.html.

Temporary Facilities

OCS sources that are considered "temporary facilities" must apply BACT to address emissions of any pollutant that would significantly affect the air quality of an onshore area.[123] Temporary facilities are defined as offshore operations in one location lasting less than three years.[124] Note that EPA's time frame for temporary is two years.

OCS Vessel Emissions

OCS vessel emissions in DOI's jurisdiction are counted the same as emissions in EPA's jurisdiction. CAA Section 328(a)(4) contains the definition for OCS source. This definition applies to sources in both EPA and DOI jurisdictions.[125] As discussed above, support vessel emissions "servicing or associated with an OCS source, including emissions while at the OCS source or en route to or from the OCS source within 25 miles of the OCS source, shall be considered direct emissions from the OCS source."

The DOI regulatory text addressing vessel emissions does not precisely match up with the CAA text. Although the activity-specific plan regulations require lessees to document support vessel emissions,[126] the exemption formula provision (discussed above) specifically points to air emissions documented under a different subsection,[127] which does not include vessel emissions. However, DOI *guidance* on emission calculations for plan submittals mirrors the statutory text.[128]

Procedural Requirements

The DOI regulations set specific time frames for agency review of Exploration Plans (EPs) and Development and Production Plans (DPPs). In general, these time frames are considerably shorter than those for EPA. These time frames are identified in **Table 5**. The maximum time frame for EP review is much shorter than for DPP review.

---

[123] 30 C.F.R. §550.303(h).

[124] 30 C.F.R. §550.302.

[125] As stated in the introductory text of §328(a)(4), the definitions apply to §328(a), which discusses EPA's program, and §328(b), which covers the OCS areas adjacent to Texas, Louisiana, Mississippi, and Alabama.

[126] 30 C.F.R. §550.224 (EP) and §550.257 (DPP).

[127] 30 C.F.R. §550.218(a) for EPs; §550.249(a) for DPPs.

[128] DOI, "Gulf of Mexico Air Emission Calculations Instructions," accompanying Form BOEM-0138.

Table 5. BOEM Review of Exploration Plans and Development and Production Plans

(time frames for different procedural steps)

Time Frames	Exploration Plan	Development and Production Plan
For BOEM to determine if a plan is deemed submitted	15 working days	25 working days
After deemed submitted, for a governor of an affected State to submit comments	21 calendar days	60 calendar days
After deemed submitted, public comment period	No public comment period	60 calendar days (concurrent with state governor time frame)
Final Decision[a]	30 calendar days after plan is deemed submitted	60 calendar days after (1) comment period closes; (2) BOEM releases its final environmental impact statement (EIS);[b] or (3) BOEM receives plan amendments

Source: 30 C.F.R. §§550.231-550.233 (EP) and §§550.266-550.270 (DPP).

a.   BOEM may (1) approve the plan; (2) require a plan modification; or (3) disapprove plan.

b.   The regulations do not require an EIS for every DPP. In general, DOI must prepare an EIS at least once in every OCS planning area (30 C.F.R. §550.269).

Coastal Zone Management Act Review

Section 307(c)(3) of the Coastal Zone Management Act (CZMA) requires lessees to certify the "consistency" of an EP or DPP with an approved coastal zone management program of an affected state (or states).[129] Section 307(f) specifically requires coordination with CAA requirements.

When a state determines that a lessee's plan is inconsistent with its coastal zone management program, the lessee must either reform its plan to accommodate those objections and resubmit it for BOEM and state approval, or succeed in appealing the state's determination to the Secretary of Commerce.[130]

Some have questioned the impact of the CZMA consistency provision.[131] Historically, states have concurred with about 95% of the federal actions they have been asked to certify. As of 2009, 43 consistency decisions have been subjects of Commerce Secretary determinations. The subject of 18 of these appeals has been offshore energy activities. However, the most recent of these decisions was rendered in 1999.[132]

---

[129] 16 U.S.C. §1456(c).

[130] 30 C.F.R. §550.235

[131] See e.g., Sam Kalen, "The BP Macondo Well Exploration Plan: Wither the Coastal Zone Management Act?," *Environmental Law Reporter*, November 2010.

[132] National Oceanic and Atmospheric Administration, Ocean and Coastal Resource Management, Appeals to the Secretary of Commerce Under the Coastal Zone Management Act (CZMA) - January 15, 2009, http://www.coastalmanagement.noaa.gov/consistency/media/appealsdecisionlist011509.pdf.

It is widely believed that the existence of the consistency requirement and the uncertainty of the outcome of an appeal have led applicants to negotiate with states and to modify proposed actions early on, thereby reducing the number of appeals. However, there are no data on the number of proposed actions that have been altered because of the consistency process.[133]

In addition, the CZMA regulations—implemented by the National Oceanic and Atmospheric Administration (NOAA)—indicate that some OCS activities may not require a review.[134] As activities occur farther offshore, a state's CZMA review authority becomes less clear. According to NOAA, a coastal state's ability to review activity-specific plans stops at the point where coastal effects are not "reasonably foreseeable." Whether this threshold is met would be determined on a case-by-case basis with the state, the lessee, and DOI.[135]

Public Participation

The DPP regulations require a 60-day comment period, in which any party may submit comments or recommendations to the BOEM Regional Supervisor.[136] The EP process does not include an opportunity for public participation (**Table 5**).

Judicial Review

The OCSLA provides opportunity for judicial review of agency action alleged to be in violation of federal law, including the OCSLA, its implementing regulations, and the terms of any permit or lease.[137]

Comparison of DOI and EPA Air Programs

Table 6 compares selected elements of the EPA and DOI air emission programs. The table examines the requirements applicable to outer OCS sources in EPA's jurisdiction. Inner OCS sources must follow the requirements that would apply to an onshore source in the corresponding onshore area. As discussed above, these provisions vary by state and whether the area is an attainment or nonattainment area. Regardless, inner OCS source requirements would be at least as stringent as outer source requirements in all situations, and potentially more stringent in some locations (e.g., California).

The primary difference between the EPA and DOI programs is rooted in the different statutory authorities: the 1990 CAA and the 1978 OCSLA. The primary objectives of these statutes are different—air quality versus offshore energy development. The two regulatory programs reflect these underlying differences.

---

[133] For more information, see CRS Report RL34339, *Coastal Zone Management: Background and Reauthorization Issues*, by Harold F. Upton; and CRS Report RL33404, *Offshore Oil and Gas Development: Legal Framework*, by Adam Vann.

[134] 15 C.F.R. Part 930.

[135] See 71 *Federal Register* 790 (January 5, 2006). See also NOAA, *CZMA Federal Consistency Overview*, February 2009.

[136] 30 C.F.R. §550.267.

[137] 43 U.S.C. §1349.

OCS sources in EPA's jurisdiction must comply with the PSD program (e.g., BACT), among other requirements. Sources subject to DOI's regime must comply with similar standards (e.g., BACT), only if their emissions would "significantly affect" a state's air quality. This key difference translates into a considerably different scope of applicability between the two programs. For example, DOI's two-step significance determination is a potentially much less stringent threshold than EPA's 250 tpy threshold for its PSD program. Moreover, the federal threshold for Title V permits is 100 tpy. For sources within 25 miles of a state's shores, the PSD and Title V thresholds may be even lower.

Another substantial difference is the time frame allotted to the agencies for reviewing a potential source's permit (EPA) or activity-specific plan (DOI). In addition, the EPA permit process allows greater opportunity for input from the public. In particular, EPA's EAB offers parties a powerful tool to compel agency review.

Some stakeholders would likely argue that the additional opportunities for public involvement in EPA's permit process help create a balance between resource development and environmental concerns. Others would likely contend these steps present unnecessary burdens and timing uncertainty in the process. If more OCS areas in EPA's jurisdiction are open for oil and gas leasing, policymakers interest in these differences will likely increase.

Table 6. EPA and DOI OCS Air Emission Programs

(comparison of selected elements)

Program Elements	EPA Outer OCS Sources Program[a]	DOI
Underlying statutory citation	1990 CAA §328 (42 U.S.C. §7627)	1978 OCSLA §5(a)(8) (43 U.S.C. §1334(a)(8))
Underlying statutory authority	Directs EPA to develop regulations requiring all OCS sources "to attain and maintain Federal and State ambient air quality standards and to comply with the provisions of [the PSD program]"	Directs DOI to develop regulations for compliance with CAA national ambient air quality standards, "to the extent that activities authorized under this subchapter significantly affect the air quality of any State"
Date of implementing regulations	September 4, 1992	March 7, 1980
Jurisdiction	All OCS sources in federal waters, except those west of 87.5 degrees longitude (the western and most of the central Gulf of Mexico) and in the federal OCS off Alaska's north coast[b]	All OCS sources in Gulf of Mexico federal waters that are west of 87.5 degrees longitude (the western and most of the central Gulf of Mexico) and OCS sources in federal waters off Alaska's north coast
Framework of requirements	Air emissions permit: PSD and/or Title V *OCS sources in EPA's jurisdiction must also submit applicable activity-specific plans per DOI regulations*[c]	Activity-specific plans: Exploration Plan (EP) or Development and Production Plan (DPP)
Emission thresholds for substantive requirements (e.g., BACT)	250 tpy	Two-step determination: (1) are emissions exempt based on distance from shore?[d] (2) if not exempt, would emissions "significantly" affect onshore air quality (as determined by modeling)?
Emission monitoring and reporting	Required for Title V permits (100 tpy threshold) and PSD permits (250 tpy threshold)	Monitoring and monthly reporting required regardless of significance determination;[e] but it is uncertain whether this is occurring

Program Elements	EPA Outer OCS Sources Program[a]	DOI
Pollutants subject to thresholds	Per PSD regulations, any "regulated pollutant,"[f] including those with a national ambient air quality standard (NAAQS): • Sulfur dioxide (SO_2) • Particulate matter ($PM_{2.5}$ and PM_{10}) • Nitrogen dioxide (NO_2) • Carbon monoxide (CO) • Ozone • Lead • Any pollutant identified as a constituent/precursor to the above (e.g., volatile organic compounds (VOC)) • Greenhouse gases (GHG)[g]	Per DOI regulations: • SO_2 • $PM_{2.5}$ and PM_{10} • Nitrogen oxide (NOx) • CO • VOC[h]
Substantive requirements if thresholds met	PSD permit requirements, including: (1) BACT (2) Air quality demonstration/analysis	If affected onshore area is an attainment area: BACT If affected onshore area is a nonattainment area: BACT and reduce all emissions with additional reductions or offsets If more than one area is impacted, the more stringent requirements would apply
Temporary source exemption	If operating for less than two years in a given location, sources are subject to BACT, but not the air quality demonstration and analyses	If operating in one location less than three years, a source must apply BACT to address emissions of any pollutant that would significantly affect the air quality of an onshore area
Other potentially applicable air emission requirements	New Source Performance Standards National Emission Standards for Hazardous Air Pollutants Title V permits *Coastal Zone Management Act Review per DOI regulations*	Activity-specific plans must include air emission information, documenting exemption Coastal Zone Management Act Review could potentially lead to air emission modifications

Program Elements	EPA Outer OCS Sources Program[a]	DOI
Time frames for agency review	PSD permit determination within 1 year of complete submittal; Title V permit within 18 months	Activity-specific plans have agency review deadlines (e.g., BOEM must provide an interim/final decision for an EP within 30 days of it being submitted)
Other federal agency involvement	EPA must consult with the applicable Federal Land Manager if a source's emissions may impact a Class I area	No analogous authority
State implementation	Coastal states may seek authority to implement and enforce EPA requirements for OCS sources in federal waters adjacent to state waters	No analogous authority
Opportunities for public participation	EPA agency must provide a 30-day public comment period when it issues a permit	BOEM must provide a 60-day public comment period for parties to review a DPP
Opportunities for administrative appeal	Environmental Appeals Board: any person can appeal an agency action	No analogous process
Opportunity for legal challenge	CAA provides opportunity for judicial review of agency actions	OCSLA provides opportunity for judicial review of agency actions

Source: Prepared by CRS.

a. Pursuant to CAA Section 328, EPA established two regulatory regimes: one for OCS sources located within 25 miles of a state's seaward boundary ("inner OCS sources"); another for OCS sources located beyond 25 miles of a state's water boundary and extending to the boundary of the EEZ ("outer OCS sources"). Requirements for "inner sources" are the same as would be applicable if the source were located in the corresponding onshore area. These requirements will vary by state and whether the corresponding onshore area is an attainment or nonattainment area for regulated pollutants.

b. P.L. 112-74 (signed by President Obama December 23, 2011) transferred air emission authority from EPA to DOI for OCS sources off Alaska's north coast.

c. The DOI activity-specific plans entail multiple provisions, including potential air emission requirements. See Notice to Lessees and Operators 2009-N11, "Air Quality Jurisdiction on the OCS," December 4, 2009.

d. For all but CO emissions, the exemption formula is: $E = 33.3D$. Thus, a source located 30 miles from shore would be exempt if its emissions were above 990 tpy.

e. This appears to apply regardless of the source's exempt status or whether the OCS source's emissions would significantly impact air quality (30 C.F.R. §550.303(k)).

f. The official term is "regulated NSR [New Source Review] pollutant," which includes (among others) any pollutant for which a national ambient air quality standard (NAAQS) has been promulgated and any pollutant identified as a constituent or precursor for a regulated NSR pollutant (40 C.F.R. §52.21(b)(50)).

g. As of January 2, 2011, an OCS source must consider its GHG emissions. These emissions are subject to a different threshold. As of July 1, 2011, new emission sources—not already subject to PSD for other pollutants—would be subject to PSD, if GHG emissions equal or exceed 100,000 tpy of carbon dioxide equivalents (CO2e). If an OCS source is already subject to PSD for one or more of the 250 tpy-threshold pollutants, the GHG emission threshold is 75,000 tpy of CO2e.

h. If VOC emissions breach the exemption threshold, they are automatically considered to "significantly" affect onshore air quality.

Author Contact Information

Jonathan L. Ramseur
Specialist in Environmental Policy
jramseur@crs.loc.gov, 7-7919